SAPPHO
Poems and Fragments

SAPPHO
Poems & Fragments

A Meadowland Book Title
Published by Carol Publishing Group

Carol Publishing Group Edition - 1993

Translation and Introduction Copyright © 1984 by Josephine Balmer
Published 1988 by Meadowland Books
By arrangement with Brilliance Books, London

A Meadowland Book Title
Published by Carol Publishing Group
Meadowland Books is a registered trademark of Carol Communications, Inc.

Editorial Offices: 600 Madison Avenue, New York, NY 10022
Sales & Distribution Offices: 120 Enterprise Avenue, Secaucus, NJ 07094
In Canada: Canadian Manda Group, P.O. Box 920, Station U, Toronto,
Ontario, M8Z 5P9, Canada

Queries regarding rights and permissions should be addressed to:
Carol Publishing Group, 600 Madison Avenue, New York, NY 10022

Manufactured in the United States of America
ISBN 0-8216-2000-2

Carol Publishing Group books are available at special discounts
for bulk purchases, for sales promotions, fund raising, or
educational purposes. Special editions can also be created to
specifications. For details contact: Special Sales Department,
Carol Publishing Group, 120 Enterprise Ave., Secaucus, NJ 07094

12 11 10 9 8 7 6 5 4 3

for Sheila

I would like to thank Sheila Andon and my family, Darlene Balmer, Edward Balmer, Paul Dunn, Teresa Trangmar and Alan Trangmar for their suggestions, support and encouragement over and above the call of duty and to acknowledge the assistance of Ruth Padel who made helpful comments on several of the translations. I am particularly grateful to Ronnie Cann who gave me a great deal of advice and devoted much time to discussing difficult texts.

CONTENTS

INTRODUCTION

Sappho and her Critics

> After his nephew had sung one of Sappho's songs over the wine, Solon of Athens, the son of Execestides, told the lad to teach it to him immediately. When someone asked why he was so eager, Solon replied, 'So that I may die knowing it.'[1]

Solon's instantaneous and uncomplicated delight in Sappho's poetry typifies the attitude of the Ancient Greeks to her work. She was considered one of their finest poets, an integral part of their cultural history. Her face was engraved on coinage, her statue erected, her portrait painted on vases. Many ancient commentators praised her literary genius, while Plato, among others, called her 'the tenth Muse'.[2]

For the modern reader Sappho's poetry can be far more difficult. Over the centuries much of her work has been lost and those poems which have survived are fragmentary – a few lines quoted in passing by later writers or pieced together from scraps of papyri excavated in Egypt. Often there is little indication of the context of the piece, of what precedes or follows. Greek literary traditions can also be alienating; the composition and performance of poetry was very different as, more importantly, were its social function and the expectations of its audience.

The greatest problem Sappho's poetry presents is its eroticism – a problem because so many translators and commentators have found it so. Sappho's reputation has changed since Solon's time; today her name is synonymous with 'unnatural sexual relations between women', as the *OED* puts it, rather than artistic excellence. Many studies of her work are preoccupied with her sexuality, with discussing whether she was 'morally pure' or a 'disturbed pervert', whether she was merely inclined towards 'inversion' or whether she practised it as well.

The feminist scholar, Mary Lefkowitz, has pointed out that these biographical obsessions are typical of the critical treatment of women writers.[3] In literary mythology, male genius derives from an overpowering urge to create, a devotion which surpasses the mundane claims of the material world and triumphs admirably over superfluous domestic ties. Female genius, on the other hand, evolves as compensation for the lack of a 'normal' domestic life – the correct outlet for women's creativity. Hence Virginia Woolf is frigid, Emily Dickinson is a frustrated spinster, Charlotte Brontë is disappointed in love and throughout history Sappho has been physically repellent (i.e. unable to attract a sexual partner), promiscuous and passionately jealous.

Because women's creativity has been so directly linked to the circumstances of their lives, their work is often regarded as autobiographical; an emotional outpouring which is divorced from literary artifice and intellectual precision. One scholar, for example, has written that Sappho's poetry has the 'air of reality, of being derived immediately and directly from Sappho's own experience'. Similarly, in a discussion of No. 32 (94*LP*) in which Sappho describes the parting dialogue of two separated lovers, he comments: 'it is not hard to believe that some conversation took place and that its substance was not entirely different from this record of it.'[4]

These comments and many like it appear to praise Sappho's work but in fact deny the strength of her poetic imagination, denigrate the artistry and subtlety of her work and ignore the importance of inherited literary and social convention. They are typical of a great many commentators who consistently project on to the text contemporary male assumptions about the nature of women's art. A more balanced assessment, as some classical scholars are beginning to argue,[5] should attempt to discard prejudices, while acknowledging the difficulties of interpretation and appreciation. It is necessary to place Sappho in her historical context, to examine the importance of her gender and sexuality and to ask what was the nature of her genius and the extent of her achievement.

Sappho and Greece

Despite the many theories, claims and counter-claims, very little is known about Sappho's life. Evidence is slight and, as is so often the case with classical history, most of the details are tentative. The main difficulty is that the oldest surviving biographical accounts were written several centuries after Sappho's death and the longest, an entry in the *Suda*, an historical and literary encyclopaedia, was written in the tenth century A.D. Piecing together all the available facts, historians agree that Sappho lived c.600B.C. on the island of Lesbos, in the eastern Aegean sea off the coast of Asia Minor (modern Turkey), probably in Mytilene, its largest city. Beyond this little else can be substantiated. Most of the sources give details about Sappho's family – parents, brothers, husband, daughter – but these cannot be proved. Her poetry mentions a daughter, Cleis, an unnamed mother and brother and it can only be assumed that these are her own. The lifestyle described in her poems suggests that she was a member of the wealthy, ruling aristocracy and this is reflected in the sources.

What sort of society did Sappho live in? In the *Iliad* and the *Odyssey*, the epic poems attributed to Homer and completed about 700B.C., an aristocratic warrior class exercises complete control. Its wealth is based on land and its society is grouped around the extended family, the *oikos*, who live on rural estates. By 600B.C. the basis of power was the city state, the *polis*, where the aristocracy still clung to a tenuous control. Greek civilization was in a period of transition, caught between the demise of the old ruling class and the rise of a new political system and consciousness, democracy. Rival family factions struggled for power and, in many cities, tyrants seized control.

Lesbos and in particular Mytilene were not immune to these troubles. The aristocracy still held power but they were a class in crisis. In the late seventh century B.C., the ruling tribe or family in Mytilene was the Penthilidae, who misused their power and clubbed their opponents to death in the street. When they were overthrown, feuding aristocratic families fought for control. The exact sequence of events is unclear and the evidence is confused. To complicate matters, from c. 610B.C. Lesbos was involved in a war with Athenian colonists at Sigeum, near Troy on the coast of Asia Minor.

There is some evidence that Sappho was involved in this turmoil. Around 600B.C. the family faction of the aristocratic male poet Alcaeus attempted to overthrow the current regime of the tyrant Myrsilus. But his fellow conspirator, Pittacus, went over to Myrsilus's camp, betrayed his companions and Alcaeus's faction was expelled. Sources note that Sappho was a contemporary of Alcaeus and Pittacus and one states that she was exiled to Sicily.[6] In her poetry she mentions some of the rival groups; the Penthilidae in No. 46 (71*LP*); the Polyanactidae in Nos 45 (155 *LP*) and 99*LP* and in

4

No. 74 (98b *LP*) the Cleanactidae. The fragmentary text of 98 also contains the word 'exile' or 'flight', although the rest of the sentence is lost and its meaning is obscure. In the poem, Sappho laments the fact that she is unable to provide her daughter with a headband from Sardis. The context of this statement may well be that Sappho is in exile and unable to obtain the luxuries of Lesbos but it is impossible to prove this conclusively.[7] What is important is that these references show that Sappho was aware of, if not involved in, contemporary political events.

One important consideration is the position of women in this period and the way in which they were affected by social changes. Aristocratic society in Lesbos was similar to that described in the Homeric epics. Fundamental to this patriarchal and militaristic culture was a sharp division between male and female activities, a delineation of their separate roles and spheres of influence. Government, trade, but mainly war were the business of men, and glory in battle their greatest achievement. Women, often the spoils or prizes of combat, were excluded from political or economic activity. Their purpose was marriage, their glory, chastity, their world, the home. 'Go home and attend to your work, to your loom and spindle,' Hector tells his wife, Andromache, in the *Iliad*, 'and see that the woman servants attend to theirs – war is the concern of men.'[8] Outside the home, religion was the only public activity in which women could participate. They supervised the cults of the female deities such as Aphrodite, Hera and Artemis and it is therefore not surprising that these figure prominently in Sappho's poetry.

Despite this role division, the evidence of Homer's poems suggests that women were less restricted than they were a few centuries later. They appear to mix freely with men, they are present at public feasts and their opinion is often sought and respected.[9] In the *Odyssey*, Odysseus prepares to visit his father. 'My house and my belongings,' he tells his wife

Penelope, 'I leave in your care.'[10] In a society in which tribal and family ties were politically important, marriage was considered desirable and a bride was respected, if only for her family connections.[11] Many commentators believe that women were particularly valued and esteemed on Lesbos.[12] To a certain extent this might be true: Sappho, at the very least, had some knowledge of political events, she was certainly educated and her poems illustrate that men and women were not totally segregated on Lesbos.

Yet the old world was vanishing. The individual warrior, for example, was being replaced by soldiers in group formation, the *phalanx*. This had a far-reaching effect on aristocratic society which was gradually transformed from a military to a leisured class.[13] Male culture remained deeply competitive but the emphasis turned from war to athletics and sport. Men began to congregate at the gymnasium and wrestling-ground and the symposium, a male drinking party, became the focus for political and social life. These changes led to an increased segregation of the sexes and the seclusion of women inside the house.

On a wider scale, the structure of society was changing, from large rural estates to the smaller households in the city state, from the extended tribal groups to self-contained nuclear families. Women were valued less and less for their family connections or for the political alliance their marriage might cement. Instead their position within their husband's family became important as well as their ability to provide sons for the inheritance of property and citizenship from which they were themselves excluded. Marriage began to be seen as a burden to men and women's sexuality thought dangerous and alarming.[14] The philosopher Solon, for example, who lived in Athens in the early sixth century B.C., was reputed to have said that a man should try to have sex with his wife at least three times a month.[15] An explicit misogyny, absent from Homer, appears in later poets.

6

Hesiod, who wrote epic poetry at the beginning of the seventh century B.C., tells the story of Pandora's box, attributing the presence of evil in the world to women, 'a bane to mortal men'. Semonides of Amorgos wrote a long invective against women in the mid-seventh century, comparing them to various unpleasant species of animals.[16]

This devaluation of women is reflected in changing attitudes to the mythical heroine, Helen of Troy. In the *Iliad*, war breaks out between Greece and Troy when Paris, a prince of Troy, steals Helen from her husband, Menelaus of Sparta. Later Greek writers found it impossible to believe that a ten-year war could be fought for the sake of a woman.[17] Significantly, Helen was an important image for Sappho who uniquely invests her with autonomous thought and action. Whether women on Lesbos were valued or not in Sappho's lifetime, it was still a society in crisis. And the outcome of this turmoil, as we have seen, brought fundamental ideological and social changes for women. It therefore seems reasonable to expect Sappho's poetry to contain responses to these changes and to reflect the increasing tension between the sexes.

Sappho and Sexuality

A few centuries after her death, Sappho's name began to be surrounded by scandal. Faced with the anomaly of a woman poet, many commentators reported that she was a prostitute, while others told apocryphal stories about her unrequited love for a ferryman, Plaon, and her subsequent suicide.[18] Much of this information originated in comic plays about Sappho written and produced at Athens in the fourth century B.C., although only a few scattered references survive.[19] These comedies probably made biographical assumptions about the eroticism of Sappho's poetry and may well have been used as a source of information by later biographers. A papyrus fragment from the second or third century A.D., for example, claims that 'some people accused' Sappho of being 'a lover of women'. Porphyrion, writing in the third century A.D., comments that Sappho was called 'masculine' either because of her poetic skill or because of her homosexuality. The entry in the *Suda* states that she had a reputation for 'shameful liaisons with women'.[20]

But the fascination for salacious details really began at Rome in the first century A.D. with the Latin poets Horace and Ovid. In Ovid's famous poem, the 'Epistle of Sappho and Phaon', later translated by Alexander Pope, Sappho relates how she once loved Anactoria, Atthis and all the other women mentioned in her poems but now she has rejected her 'shameful' past for the love of a man, Phaon: 'what once belonged to many women,' she tells him, 'now you alone possess.'[21] The concept of vicious forbidden love, of shame and guilt and the rejection of a deviant lifestyle for a man who does not love her all became standard features of the mythology of Sappho.

This image was adopted in particular by nineteenth-century French writers, obsessed by decadent sexuality. In Baudelaire's poem 'Lesbos', Sappho indulges in lurid frenzied relationships with women until she is overcome by her passion for Phaon. Verlaine's poem 'Sappho' follows a similar pattern. Pierre Louÿs' semi-pornographic work, *Les Chansons de Bilitis*, appeared in 1895 and contained the familiar description of life on Lesbos; Bilitis, a newcomer to the island, is seduced on arrival by Sappho. Gradually, through the work of these and other writers, Sappho had become a sexual rather than a literary celebrity.

Classical scholars were horrified by these portraits of Sappho. One, Wilamowitz, was so outraged by Louÿs' inferences in particular that he immediately rushed to Sappho's defence. In his book, *Sappho und Simonides*,

8

published in 1913, he repudiated all claims that Sappho was a sexual deviant. Instead, he said, she was a wife and mother, a paragon of womanly virtues. He noticed that a few ancient commentators referred to the women in Sappho's poetry as her 'pupils' and claimed that she was the leader of a formal cult at Lesbos, dedicated to the worship of Aphrodite. The women in her poems were young initiates whose literary and moral education she supervised. But his sources were highly suspect; the main piece of evidence, a comment by Maximus of Tyre that Sappho's relationship with the women in her poems was similar to the philosopher/teacher Socrates' relationship with his male following, is extremely ambiguous.[22]

Although Wilamowitz's views are no longer fashionable, some modern scholars are still influenced by them. C.M. Bowra, for example, in his book *Greek Lyric Poetry* (1961) writes that it is wrong to compare Sappho's poetry to that of the male homosexual poets, although 'in later times . . . Sappho's emotions were misjudged and hard names were given to her'.[23] Judith Hallett, in a recent article in *Signs*, claims that Sappho held a 'formal' position at Lesbos which she links to the segregation of the sexes. She denies Sappho's lesbianism and sees her as a 'sensual consciousness raiser' whose poetry is a 'social vehicle for imparting sensual awareness and sexual self-esteem to women on the threshold of marriage and maturity'.

In general, recent commentators concede that many of Sappho's poems are passionate expressions of love between women. Yet most scholars are still worried about the nature of this passion. Albin Lesky, for example, states that Sappho's love is a 'desire for spiritual domination' and that 'there is nothing to suggest that it had any base origin'. Denys Page comments that Sappho's poetry displays 'a lover's passion' as well as 'an overwhelming emotion of the intensest love' but concludes that there is no evidence to suggest 'practice as well as inclination'. The anthropologist George Devereux takes this discussion a stage further. He decides that Sappho was a 'masculine lesbian' with a 'clinically commonplace female castration complex'.[24]

The application of these theories to Sappho's text results in some strange readings of her poetry. No. 20 (31LP), in particular, has been subjected to some unusual interpretations. Wilamowitz, faced with such sensual writing, explained that it was a wedding song performed at the marriage of Sappho's favourite pupil. 'That man' is the bridegroom and Sappho's emotion is sorrow at being parted from the girl. Page refutes this theory but, like many other male scholars, sees the man as the focus of interest. Sappho, he claims, feels passionate jealousy towards the man who is favoured by the woman she loves.[25]

George Devereux cites the poem as evidence of Sappho's homosexuality which he sees as a pathological condition. She is not jealous of the man, he writes, because she cannot help but identify with his masculinity. She finds him 'equal to the gods' because he has something which she cannot offer the woman – it is all a simple case of phallus envy. Devereux concludes that Sappho's emotions affect her so violently because her 'girlfriend is taken away from her not by another lesbian but by a *man* who has what she does not have and what she would give her life to have'.[26]

In search of evidence to support their theories, scholars scour Sappho's poems for references which could be construed as conclusive either way. Judith Hallett, attempting to prove that Sappho was exclusively heterosexual, notes that she had a daughter (No. 75 [132LP]), while others point to No. 41 (121LP) in which marriage with a younger man is discussed. For the other side, four lines are presented which are said to contain explicit proof of physical contact: No. 4 (46LP), No. 12 (126LP), No. 32 1.22 (94LP) and No. 47 (213LP). One fragment, which seems to include the word '*olisbos*', the Greek word for a leather phallus, has been adopted as evidence by both camps (99*LP*).

But the real difficulty is not the evidence but attitudes towards it. Sappho's poems are not autobiographical tracts and should not be treated as such. First there is the consideration of poetic persona, of the subtle and complex use of 'I' in poetry. The transformation of experience into art is rarely straightforward and although Sappho's own voice is certainly representative of personal feelings, it is also governed by literary conventions and by the intentions of her poetry. There is also the practical problem. It is impossible to ascertain the context of many fragments, especially the shorter pieces; they might well be part of reported speech or dialogue as in Nos 39 (137*LP*), 78 (1*LP*) and 61 (109*LP*), for example, or even from an account of a mythological story as in Nos 97 (142*LP*) and 88 (54*LP*).[27]

Scholars who attempt to 'explain' or classify Sappho's eroticism in pedantic, clinical terms refer only to contemporary thought. But what was the attitude of the Greeks and how was it reflected in Sappho's poetry? As we have seen, segregation and a sharp division of sexual roles led to women's sexuality becoming an object of fear for Greek men. Women are thought to have a larger sexual appetite than men and heterosexual sex to rob men of their virility.[28] The story of Actaeon, who was torn to pieces by his own hounds when he caught sight of the goddess Artemis bathing, illustrates the strong taboo against female nudity.[29] In the seventh and sixth centuries B.C., votive statues of young men, *kouroi*, depicted nude figures, whereas those of women, *korai*, were clothed.[30] Historians link increased segregation, the growing exclusiveness of male culture and the emphasis on male prowess in war, with male homosexuality and concede that in aristocratic Greek society it was considered not only acceptable but desirable; the male rather than the female form was thought to be the embodiment of beauty, love between men, the romantic ideal.[31]

It is also often inferred that aristocratic Greek women, neglected and despised before and after marriage, imitated male society and turned to their own sex for physical gratification, almost as a last resort.[32] Certainly, as well as Sappho's poetry, there is other evidence which refers to love between women and some which links it with Lesbos. The male poet Anacreon who lived on the mainland of Asia Minor in the sixth century B.C., describes how the woman he loves ignores him because 'she is from Lesbos and gapes after another woman'.[33] An early sixth-century plate from Thera and an Attic red figure vase c. 500B.C. show women 'courting'[34] and arousing each other. An epitaph from Athens dating from the late fifth century B.C. also records the love of two women:

Because of the truth and sweetness of your love,
your companion, Euthylla, placed this stone
on your grave, Biote; she remembers you
forever in her tears and weeps for the youth
you have lost.[35]

Perhaps the most important reference to female homosexuality is in Plato's *Symposium*, written in the early fourth century B.C. At a drinking party each guest is called on to make a speech about love. The comic playwright Aristophanes relates a spurious myth to explain sexual longing; once people were double beings but when they angered the gods, they were split in two. Now they long to be complete again. Those who were once a man and a woman seek each other out, as do those who were once two men and those who were once two women; for it is only in the sexual act that they can temporarily regain their wholeness.[36] Plato's attitude is singularly lacking in moral judgement; to him, sexual preference was merely a matter of chance.

Sappho's work has a similar shamelessness and lack of self-consciousness. Her poetry is sensual and emotional rather than sexually explicit. The erotic intensity of her work is well illustrated by No. 32 (94LP), in which she describes a parting from and memory of a loved companion. All attention is centred on the absent woman and, in particular, on her body: Sappho tells us that her friend sat by her side; that she wove garlands around her neck – in vase painting a common feature of homosexual courtship; that she anointed herself, which was usually done while naked after a bath; and finally that she satisfied her desire. The description of their surroundings is also imbued with sensuality: the various flowers; the rich perfume; the soft bed; the stream. Sappho heightens the emotional strength of the poem by creating an imaginary world of memory, occupied only by herself and her lost lover.[37] In the context of this coherent poetic focus it seems trite and redundant to ask whether 'the girls of Lesbos . . . sought to induce orgasms in one another by bodily contact'.[38] Rather more important is the internal poetic meaning of Sappho's sensuality and exclusive concern for women.

In male Greek poetry, desire for women is expressed in vague terms. Romantic intensity is reserved for relationships between men. These are traditionally described in terms of military combat, as a hopelessly imbalanced struggle for domination with one partner, the *eromenos* or loved one, inexorably running away from the other, the *erastes* or lover. Some scholars claim that Sappho's erotic concentration on women illustrates the transference of dominant male values to the world of women.[39] But this view represents a fundamental misunderstanding of her poetic intentions. No. 78 (1LP), for example, in which Aphrodite is summoned for help in a love affair, certainly echoes male conventions; Sappho calls Aphrodite her *summachos*, her ally in battle, and begs her not to allow her heart to be subjugated or conquered. In the sixth stanza, in particular, flight, pursuit and the giving of gifts are all elements of formalized male relationships.[40] Yet in Sappho's poems, this exchange is not static; roles will be reversed, beloved will soon be lover and vice versa. Love between women is not a matter of domination and subordination – their desire is mutual and equal.[41] Using the framework of male literary conventions, Sappho creates an alternative world in which a set of female values are asserted in direct opposition to those expressed in male culture. In this poetic world, desire between women, sensuality and an appreciation of female beauty do not represent an imitation or transférence but a rejection of male values and a response to the increasing devaluation of women and fear of their sexuality.

Sappho and Poetry

After asking, 'Is Sappho fit to read?' J.A.Davison, like many other critics, turns to consider the question, 'Is she worth reading?' Although most scholars eventually answer in the affirmative, a brief survey of their comments suggest that it is a close-run thing. Denys Page, for example, writes that No. 33 (96*LP*) is 'devoid of anything profound in thought or emotion or memorable in language'. Most believe that Sappho's poetry derives directly from her own experience and therefore decide that her language is 'simple' or 'homely', her style, 'unadorned with literary artifice'. Often, we are told, her emotion proves stronger than her art; she is carried away by a flight of fancy, an irrelevant train of thought or an unsuitable image. Alternatively, it is said that she uses conventional settings – a farewell speech or a prayer – as a backcloth for a descriptive piece with no ulterior poetic design.[42]

Most of these scholars ignore the difficulties involved in

appreciating Sappho's poetry. To begin with, sixth-century Greece was an oral culture and poetry was performed to an audience. Furthermore, it was not spoken but sung or recited to musical accompaniment. This convention created its own needs such as the repetition of key words, a fluency of thought, a logical movement of expression and a powerful climax, all of which can be found in No. 78 (1*LP*), the prayer to Aphrodite, Sappho's only complete surviving poem.

Similarly, the lyric form, used by Sappho and her contemporaries, was still in its infancy. Earlier Greek poetry, the *Iliad* and the *Odyssey* for example, had been epic. But in the seventh century a new type of poetry emerged, the lyric, which was short, personal and spoke directly to its audience about individual emotions. There were different kinds of lyric, including the choral, sung by a choir at a formal ceremony, such as a religious festival or wedding, and the monodic, favoured by Sappho, which was sung by a single voice and was more personal in subject matter. The youth and freshness of the lyric genre should always be considered in any judgement of Sappho's work. In No. 112 (34*LP*), for example, she calls the moon 'silver', which is an extremely ordinary analogy by modern standards, common in the popular literature of romance. Yet ancient commentators praise Sappho for this comparison and record that she was the first to use it. This point might seem obvious in studies of, say, Shakespeare, many of whose metaphors have become part of everyday speech, but has often been overlooked in those of Greek poetry.

Another problem is that little is known about the performance of Sappho's poetry. Some scholars believe that all of her poems were designed to be presented at a cult ceremony while others argue that she performed them privately on informal occasions. Scholars also dispute whether her audience consisted of both men and women or whether they were exclusively female. The only reference in Sappho's extant work to the performance of her poetry is No. 98 (160*LP*), which seems to suggest that at least some of her poems were sung to a private audience of her women companions. Her marriage songs were obviously performed at weddings, some by a choir. There is also evidence that some of the fragments had their origins in cultic worship, particularly No. 95 (140a*LP*) in which young women are invited to mourn the death of Adonis, the beautiful young lover of Aphrodite whose worship had arrived in Lesbos from the East. All in all, it seems reasonable to suppose that Sappho's poetry served not one but a variety of purposes.

Finally there is the question of Sappho's position as a woman poet. A.R.Burn has commented that Sappho appears to take this for granted and argues that on Lesbos in particular, but elsewhere in Greece as well, poetry was a common pursuit of women.[43] There are references in Sappho's poetry to the poetic skill of her friends; in No. 22 (22*LP*), for example, she invites Gongyla to 'take up your lyre and sing for us' and here, as in many other fragments, the practice of poetry is linked with desire. The ancient sources contain information about several women poets from other parts of Greece, some of whose poetry still survives. But even in antiquity their work was often denigrated. Praxilla, who lived in Sicyon in the fifth century B.C., was famous for the silliness of her poetry. There is also a story which tells how Corinna, who is thought to have also lived in the fifth century, defeated the male poet Pindar in several poetry competitions, although her victory is imputed not to her poetic skill but to her outstanding beauty which is said to have swayed the judges.[44] A surviving fragment of Corinna's verse scolds another woman poet, Myrtis, for competing with Pindar, 'although she is only a woman' and this illustrates that women writers themselves felt far from confident about their work.[45]

The first charges made against Sappho's work by modern

scholars is that her language and style are prosaic and simplistic. She records events as they are, as they have happened to her, it is said, and makes no attempt to display an artistic discernment. No. 33 (96LP), for example, has been the subject of many criticisms. Scholars are worried by the central image of the poem which compares a woman absent in Sardis to the moon and extends the simile to include a description of the natural world over which the moonlight falls. Some critics believe that the moon and woman are mutually identified; as the moon sheds its light over the sea and fields, so does the woman.[46] Others argue that, instead, the moon and the woman are contrasted; the calm of the moon is placed in opposition to the restless grief of the absent lover.[47]

But most commentators see the image and subsequent description as a literary red herring. Denys Page writes that the moon begins as a symbol of the woman's beauty but rapidly becomes nothing more than a charming digression which has little to do with the rest of the poem.[48] Richard Jenkyns also adopts this attitude and believes that Sappho's account is nothing more than a catalogue of names.[49] Such comments fail to grasp the essence of Sappho's art. Her images cannot be decoded or exchanged for another single meaning nor do her descriptive passages focus on objects at random. Instead she is concerned with a wholeness, with a unity of expression. In No. 33, the extended simile exhibits an overall richness, a sense of ripeness and weight which is echoed in each of the objects mentioned; the sea is filled with salt, the fields with flowers; the dew moistens the earth and the blossom blooms. This impression links the woman with the natural world for her heart also is 'heavy with grief '.

Many scholars have been puzzled by Sappho's use of the epithet 'rose-fingered' to describe the moon in this poem. Homer applied the phrase to the dawn and this has been interpreted as a reference to the red light which streaks across the sky as the sun rises. Some critics claim that Sappho's description must mean there is a 'rosy glow' around the moon and most assume that rose equals red in colour.[50] But it makes far more sense to assume that Sappho refers to a white rose, to the white light of the moon. This is reflected in the remainder of the simile, for each of the other elements of the night are also white in colour; stars, salt, dew and flowers – roses, chervil (cow parsley) and honey-clover (white meliot).

Again these images connect Sappho's description of the moonlit night with the woman in Sardis. Ancient commentators report that Sappho loved the rose and used it in her poetry to express her appreciation of female beauty.[51] In Ancient Greece this was often associated with pale skin; on vases, for example, women's bodies were painted in white. Through the image of the rose, the woman, the moon, the flowers and night are mutually associated. Sappho further identifies the woman with the natural world by interweaving some of her favourite descriptive adjectives, usually applied to her companions, between the two; the chervil, for example, is 'delicate', the woman's heart, 'tender' and the dew, 'beautiful'.

A similar unity may be found in No. 79 (2LP) in which Aphrodite is summoned to her sacred temple and grove on Lesbos. Here Sappho is concerned with creating a sense of atmosphere; the grove she describes is not necessarily a real place at any given time but an imaginary paradise which reflects and contains Sappho's vision of Aphrodite. The season – Spring; the garden setting; the apples – a symbol of fertility and Aphrodite's own fruit; the flowers – again roses; the horses; the soft breezes and the drowsiness are all highly erotic. The description is also extremely sensual, containing references to sight, touch (the breezes and the cups), sound (the murmuring streams and rustling leaves), smell (the burning frankincense and the blossom) and taste (the nectar).[52] But Sappho is concerned with the spiritual as well as the sensual. Each exotic element of the grove echoes the cult of the goddess it houses. Through the strength of Sappho's imagery, the place of worship and the experience of worship become inseparable. Sappho's poetic skill here and elsewhere lies in a strict control of subject, a tension between language and emotion and a resonance of image. Her powerful and direct style might well be 'simple' but in its simplicity it is also extremely sophisticated.

Sappho and Women

The subject and themes of Sappho's poetry have been criticized in much the same way as her language and style. Modern scholars report rather scathingly that her poems are mostly concerned with the minutiae of daily existence, with 'trivia', 'tittle-tattle' and 'back-biting'. Denys Page, for example, writes that her principal themes are the 'ephemeral pleasures and pains of an idle but graceful society'. He points to a 'narrow limitation of interests' and claims that more serious matters than those discussed in her poetry must be left to 'more reflective minds on graver occasions'.[53]

As ever, belief in the autobiographical nature of Sappho's poetry prejudices appreciation of her work; critics claim that in her poems she is 'bitchy' or 'gossipy', that the women she 'sneers at' are leaders of rival associations or friends who have deserted her group for another. In this context, the lines 'I do not have a spiteful temper/but a tender heart' (No. 10 (120LP)) have been quoted with irony. Scholars also note that Sappho is excessively concerned with the fripperies of fashion. Albin Lesky writes that in No. 72 (44LP), Sappho 'betrays' her 'female heart' by her description of Andromache's dowry. Again, in a discussion of No. 74 (see above, page 5), Lesky states that Sappho's juxtaposition of 'the politics of her menfolk' with her interest in fashionable headgear, 'delightfully illustrates her exclusive and immediate concern with the feminine'.[54]

In one sense, Lesky is correct – Sappho is exclusively concerned with the world of women, with their everyday life and ocupations; 'mother, dear', she writes in No. 40 (102LP), 'I cannot weave my cloth'. Many of her poems describe religious cults which, as we have seen, were important to women – their only opportunity to participate in public life. But Lesky's comments, intended to expose Sappho's frivolity, serve only to trivialize the intentions of her work. They illustrate a bias against women's art, a contempt for women's experience and a firm belief that there are more suitable subjects for serious literature. Sappho's poems do contain references to clothing (cf. No. 22 [22LP]; No. 24 [100LP] and No. 25 [39LP]) but these are not fashion bulletins. Instead, Sappho draws attention to women's clothing and hence their bodies as an expression of her sensual appreciation of female beauty. Again, in No. 74, her purpose is not to discuss the availability and purchase of headbands but to portray the relationships of mothers and daughters over three generations.

Another poem which celebrates love between mother and daughter has been described by Richard Jenkyns as 'charming but slight'.[55]

I have a beautiful daughter, golden
like a flower, my beloved Cleis,
for her, in her place, I would not accept
the whole of Lydia, nor lovely . . . (No. 75 [132LP])

But far from being 'slight' this small fragment expresses one of the main concerns of Sappho's poetry. To the inhabitants of Lesbos, the kingdom of Lydia, their neighbour on the mainland of Asia Minor, represented wealth, power and luxury. It was a country with extensive natural resources and was also a centre for trade. During Sappho's lifetime, Alyattes, the Lydian king, extended its frontiers by military conquest and began to amass a vast personal fortune. Sappho's rejection of Lydia for Cleis represents a preference for the experience of women over the male world of politics, trade and war. The image appears again in No. 21 (16LP); for Sappho, beauty rests in the sight of Anactoria's face rather than Lydian chariots and so it is Anactoria she loves and values, desire between women she asserts over the male concept of military glory.[56]

The poems which Sappho wrote for performance at wedding ceremonies also illustrate her concern with women's experience. As we have seen, marriage was considered a woman's sole purpose, the height of her achievement, but gradually her role within it became devalued. In the work of male poets such as Semonides and Hesiod, wives are characterized as shrewish, lazy, greedy and promiscuous. The only positive advantages of 'acquiring' a wife were the heirs she might bear and the work she would do, providing she was carefully trained and her disposition proved suitably malleable.[57] In Sappho's wedding songs emphasis is laid on the qualities of the bride and the good fortune of the groom. In No. 63 (113LP), she tells the groom that 'no woman was ever lovelier' than his bride. In addition, men in her poems are eager for marriage; in No. 62 (112LP), the groom has 'prayed' for his marriage and 'dreamed' of his bride. Sappho understood the significance of marriage for women. She reaffirms their importance within the marriage partnership, the value of their contribution and characterizes relations between husband and wife in terms of mutual love and respect, not fear and hatred.

Linked to Sappho's poems on love and marriage are those concerned with virginity. In Greek society, chastity was a symbol of female honour and some of Sappho's poems reflect this: 'I will remain a virgin/for ever,' she writes in No. 70

(152*E*). But society also insisted that women should marry and have children, that their virginity should be surrendered:

> [Why am I unhappy?]
> Am I still longing
>
> > for my lost virginity? (No. 69
> > [107*LP*])

Sappho stresses the physical trauma of loss of virginity but more importantly her poems symbolize the emotional trauma of marriage and its effect on women's lives – the separation from family and friends and the move from their own home to the strange surroundings of their husband's house and family.[58]

A poem by Alcaeus, Sappho's male contemporary, describes the marriage of the mythical Peleus and Thetis: 'he took her from the halls of Nereus to the home of Chiron; he unclasped the pure virgin's girdle and the love between Peleus and the best of Nereus' daughters was consummated.'[59] Thetis's role is passive. She is not even mentioned by name but identified only by her chastity and by her father's name. In comparison, Sappho's poetry is startling; by focusing entirely on the reactions of women to virginity and its loss, on their sense of honour, their distress and sorrow, she animates their experiences and takes them far beyond the dumb, shadowy figures of Alcaeus.

Another interesting point of comparison between Alcaeus's poem and Sappho's work is their contrasting attitudes to Helen of Troy. Alcaeus compares the 'wicked deeds' of Helen, which, he believes, were responsible for the destruction of Troy, to the virtue of Thetis who remained faithful to her husband and whose son, Achilles, was instrumental in the downfall of the city. Alcaeus's view is derived from Homer; in the *Iliad*, Helen is blamed for the war between Greece and Troy and is shunned and despised by many Trojans. Furthermore, she voices her own shame at her elopement with Paris, calling herself 'evil-minded and detestable'. In one passage she weeps as she remembers her home and the family, parents, husband and daughter she has left behind.[60]

Sappho makes no moral judgement on Helen. In No. 21 she asks the question 'what is the loveliest sight on earth?' and answers that it is subjective – 'whatever you desire'. Helen is cited as an example to prove the point. Sappho refutes Homer's claim that Helen was ashamed of her actions and longed to go home and defiantly tells us, echoing Homer's exact words, that Helen forgot all the ties which bound her to Sparta. In Homer, Helen is passive; she is first abducted by Paris, lives in misery in Troy and is finally reclaimed by the victorious Greeks as a prize of war. Sappho's Helen has a will of her own. She is not stolen like an inanimate object but deliberately leaves Sparta and sails away to Troy. Paris is not even mentioned. Helen is no longer a puppet of kings but a woman who makes her own decisions, who desires and acts on that desire, forsaking her traditional role as daughter, wife and mother. For these reasons, Page duBois has described this poem as 'one of the few texts which breaks the silence of women in antiquity, an instant in which women become more than the object of men's desire'.[61]

Sappho does not reject or even criticize the accepted place of women within her society. But the tension between male and female experience implicit in her poems reflects the changing status of women. In reality this tension was resolved by the devaluation of women and a restriction of their freedom. Sappho's poetry creates an alternative world in which aspects of women's lives are celebrated and a preference for their concerns is expressed. This preoccupation with women, which has troubled so many scholars, is unique in classical literature. Far from a source of weakness, it is closely linked to Sappho's poetic achievement, to her passionate sensuality, her exploration of beauty and desire and her concentration on the emotions of the lover, all of which had a profound influence on subsequent literature. At least the Greeks were in no doubt:

Wherever you are, lady, equal of the gods, greetings;
for we still have your immortal daughters, your songs.[62]

Notes

Abbreviations used in Introduction and Notes:

LP = Lobel, Edgar et Page, Denys (eds), *Poetarum Lesbiorum Fragmenta*, (Oxford 1955, repr. 1963)
E = Edmonds, J.M. (ed.), *Lyra Graeca Vol. I*, Loeb Classical Library, (London 1928)
PMG = *Poetae Melici Graeci*, Page, Denys (ed.), (Oxford 1962)

1   Aelian, quoted by Stobaeus, *Anthology* 3.29.58.
2   *Palatine Anthology* 9.506.
3   'Critical Stereotypes and the Poetry of Sappho', Lefkowitz, pp. 59–68.
4   Bowra, pp. 187,192.
5   See especially McEvilley and 'Advice on How to Read Sappho', Lefkowitz, pp. 69–70.
6   *Suda* iv 322s; Eusebius, *Chronicle* 01.45.1; Strabo 13.2.3; *Parian Marble* Ep.36.
7   See Page, p. 102, note on ll.7–9.
8   *Iliad* 6.490–2.
9   In the *Odyssey*, Odysseus and Nausicaa converse freely (6.110–315), although Nausicaa is worried that her reputation will be damaged if she is seen with a strange man. She also advises

Odysseus to supplicate himself before her mother, Queen Arete, rather than her father, King Alcinous, because her opinion is influential (6.310–15).

10 *Odyssey* 23.355.
11 See Pomeroy, p. 34, who cites Herodotus's account of the competition for the hand in marriage of Agariste, the daughter of Cleisthenes, tyrant of Sicyon, 600–570B.C. (Herodotus 6.126–31).
12 See J.A.Symonds, quoted by Page, pp. 140–2; Pomeroy, p. 55; Bowra, p. 178.
13 See Murray, pp. 192–208.
14 Hesiod, *Theogony* 603–12.
15 Plutarch, *Life of Solon* 20.3.
16 Hesiod, *Works and Days* 54–105; *Theogony* 567–612.
17 Herodotus 2.112–20; see Pomeroy, pp. 17–18.
18 *Suda* iv 323; Strabo 10.2.9.
19 Athenaeus 10.450e; 11.487a; 8.399c; 13.572c.
20 Porphyrion on Horace, *Epistles* 1.19.28. *Suda* iv 322s; P. Oxy 1800 fr. 1.
21 Ovid, *Heroides* 15.20.
22 Wilamowitz, p. 56ff; Maximus of Tyre 18.9.
23 Bowra, pp. 178, 238.
24 Lesky, p. 146; Page, pp. 143–4; Devereux, p. 22.
25 Wilamowitz, p. 56ff; Page, p. 28ff.
26 Devereux, p. 22.
27 See Tsagarakis, pp. 69–82, for a detailed discussion of Sappho's use of the first person.
28 Hesiod, frag 275, relates a myth in which Tiresias, who had been both male and female, is asked to solve a dispute between Zeus and Hera, the king and queen of the gods, about who enjoyed sex more, men or women. Tiresias replied that women enjoyed it nine times more than men. See also Murray, p 204
29 Tiresias was also said to have been struck blind because he saw the goddess Athena bathing. See also the story of Gyges and Candaules, Herodotus 1.8–12.
30 See Pomeroy, p. 47.
31 See Murray, pp. 204–8.
32 Ibid. pp. 149,204.
33 Anacreon 358*PMG*.

34 In Greek vase painting, 'courtship' was depicted by chin-chucking, the wearing or carrying of garlands and the exchange of gifts.

35 *Inscriptiones Graecae II²* 10954, see Lefkowitz and Fant, No. 25.

36 Plato, *Symposium* 191e.

37 See McEvilley for a full discussion of imagination and memory in this fragment.

38 Dover, p. 182.

39 See Murray, p. 149.

40 See Marry.

41 See Dover, p. 177.

42 Davison, p. 226; Page, pp. 95,30,83,91ff.

43 Burn, p. 229.

44 Praxilla: Zenobius 4.21; Corinna: Pausanias 9.22.3.

45 Corinna 664a*PMG*.

46 See Bowra, p. 195.

47 See Campbell (3), p. 16; Page, pp. 93–6.

48 Page, p. 94.

49 Jenkyns, p. 68.

50 See Page, p. 90, note on l.8; Jenkyns, p. 68; Campbell (1), p. 280, note on l.8.

51 Philostratus Ep.51.

52 See Campbell (3), p. 17.

53 Page, pp. 133,110,56.

54 Lesky, pp. 142,140.

55 Jenkyns, p. 72.

56 See duBois for a full discussion of this fragment.

57 Hesiod, *Works and Days* 695–705.

58 See Arthur, p. 72.

59 Alcaeus 42*LP*.

60 *Iliad* 24.762–75; 6.344–8; 3.173–6.

61 duBois, p. 89.

62 *Palatine Anthology* 7.407: Dioscorides on Sappho.

TRANSLATING SAPPHO

Transcribing the poetry of one language into that of another is obviously a difficult task. But as well as the subtleties and nuances of language, the translator of Sappho is faced with several technical problems. Although more than 200 fragments of her work survive, only one of these (No. 78 [1*LP*]) is complete. Many consist of a few letters or even a series of half-lines where the papyrus has been torn into strips. Some are so incomplete that it is impossible to attempt a translation of them. In addition, damaged or worn papyri mean that the reading of certain words or phrases is ambiguous and a great deal of scholarship is devoted to ascertaining exactly what Sappho might have written.

Ancient commentators praised the smoothness of Sappho's style, the 'euphony' of her language, the choice and juxtaposition of her words. Unfortunately this quality is one of the most difficult to capture when translating from one language to another, particularly from Greek to English: Greek has a far more flexible word order than English, a greater ability to mark emphasis, to use assonance or alliteration or to suggest ambiguity. In antiquity Sappho was also famous for her skilful and innovative use of metre. Again this is extremely difficult, if not impossible, to render into English as metre in

Greek poetry is measured by length, in English, by stress.

Despite these difficulties, the aim of my translations is to reproduce Sappho's poetry as faithfully as possible and each is the result of careful study of both text and critical readings. In the past, translators of Sappho have suffered from three main faults: a desire to pad out the fragments with interpretations of their own, often without indicating where they have done so; a coyness about Sappho's eroticism; and lastly a tendency to trivialize the power of Sappho's language by using trite or flowery words and phrases, traditionally associated with women's writing. All three are misleading and irritating to general reader and student alike. In order that Sappho's voice should be heard and not my own, I have not attempted to fill in the gaps in the fragments unless absolutely necessary and then I have indicated where I have done so with brackets. Most of these speculations are based on the comments of ancient writers who quoted Sappho or interpretations generally accepted by classical scholars. With the slightly longer fragments, I have attempted to retain the original form of the poem although to keep the fluency of Sappho's Greek, I have not adhered to this rigidly. I have also tried to capture, without embellishment, the sensuality of Sappho's poetry, the clarity and strength of her style, the ease of her expression and the logical progression of her thought. In short, by preserving the form, content and tone of the original Greek poems, I have attempted to allow Sappho to speak for herself.

Key to the Translations

[ ]   denotes a conjectural meaning

. . .   denotes a break in the fragment

*****   denotes the end of a fragment

The text used is *Poetarum Lesbiorum Fragmenta* ed. Edgar Lobel et Denys Page (Oxford 1955, repr. 1963).

— I —
LOVE

1

Love shook my heart
like the wind on the mountain
rushing over the oak trees

★★★★★

2

Love makes me tremble yet again
sapping all the strength from my limbs;

bittersweet, undefeated creature –
against you there is no defence

★★★★★

3

Stand up and look at me face to face,
                              friend to friend;
unfurl the loveliness in your eyes

★★★★★

4

On a soft cushion
                    I will soothe my tired body

★★★★★

5

[I ran after you]
  like a small child
              flying
                        to her mother

★★★★★

6

I tell you;
              in time to come,
someone will remember us

★★★★★

7

[From our love]
 I want neither
 the sweetness of honey
                              nor the sting of the bees

★★★★★

8

I do not expect
                      to touch the sky

★★★★★

9

[My advice to you is:]
 don't disturb
                      the jetsam
                                    [on the beach]

★★★★★

10

I do not have a spiteful temper
                                    but a tender heart

★★★★★

11

Beautiful women,
my feelings for you
will never falter

★★★★★

12

May you sleep on the breast
of your tender companion

★★★★★

13

Night crept up on them
black sleep closed their eyes

★★★★★

14

. . . for whenever I look at you,
it seems to me that not even
Hermione is your equal;
no, far better to compare you
to Helen, whose hair was golden . . .

★★★★★

15

I do not believe
            the light of day will ever see
another woman,
            now, or in time to come, who will
rival you in skill

★★★★★

16

. . . bind together, Dicca, with your slender hands, shoots
of dill,
wreathe garlands around your lovely hair;
for the Graces favour a woman crowned with blossom
but turn away from those who go ungarlanded . . .

★★★★★

17

Mnasidica,
more lovely even
than slender Gyrinno

★★★★★

18

. . . Atthis,
 for you . . .

★★★★★

19

. . . for you, I will leave behind
 [all that I love . . .]

★★★★★

– II –
DESIRE

It seems to me that man is equal to the gods,
that is, whoever sits opposite you
and, drawing nearer, savours, as you speak,
the sweetness of your voice

and the thrill of your laugh, which have so stirred the heart
in my own breast, that whenever I catch
sight of you, even if for a moment,
then my voice deserts me

and my tongue is struck silent, a delicate fire
suddenly races underneath my skin,
my eyes see nothing, my ears whistle like
the whirling of a top

and sweat pours down me and a trembling creeps over
my whole body, I am greener than grass,[†]
at such times, I seem to be no more than
a step away from death;

but all can be endured since even a pauper . . .

★★★★★

[†]*greener than grass*: this phrase has caused many scholars a great deal of difficulty. It is often translated as 'paler than grass' and thought to refer to the colour draining from the speaker's face. Greek colour terms are far vaguer than those in English; the adjective *chloros* could mean both brilliant green and pale yellow. However, it was used to describe the rich colour of foliage and, as Lefkowitz has argued, may well be an echo of the Homeric phrase 'green fear' which refers to the warrior's fear in battle.

Some an army of horsemen, some an army on foot
and some say a fleet of ships is the loveliest sight
on this dark earth; but I say it is what-
ever you desire:

and it is possible to make this perfectly clear
to all; for the woman who far surpassed all others
in her beauty, Helen, left her husband –
the best of all men –

behind and sailed far away to Troy; she did not spare
a single thought for her child nor for her dear parents
but [the goddess of love] led her astray
[to desire . . .]

        [. . . which]
reminds me now of Anactoria
although far away,

whose long-desired footstep, whose radiant, sparkling face
I would rather see before me than the chariots
of Lydia or the armour of men
who fight wars on foot . . .

★★★★★

[. . . come here tonight,] I beg, you, Gongyla,
take up your lyre [and sing to us;]
for once again an aura of desire
hovers around

your beauty, your dress thrills all those who see you
and the heart in my breast quickens;
once I too poured scorn on Aphrodite,
goddess of love,

but now I pray [that you will soon be here . . .]
I wish [we were never apart . . .]

★★★★★

†This poem is very fragmentary and the text is corrupt.

[Her voice was]
   far sweeter than any flute . . .
[her hair,]
   more golden than gold . . .
[and her skin,]
   far whiter than an egg . . .

★★★★★

24

And wrapped around her . . .
     a soft linen robe

★★★★★

25

      And on her feet
bright coloured sandals,
skilful Lydian work . . .

★★★★★

26

You've come and you –

                  oh, I was longing for you –

have cooled my heart

                 which was burning with desire

★★★★★

27

[I want you to know;]
  I prayed that for us

             the night

                    could last twice as long

★★★★★

28

[I was dreaming of you but]
  just then
  Dawn, in her golden sandals
              [woke me]

★★★★★

− III −
DESPAIR

. . . I know it is true;

> those that I love best
> do me the most harm . . .

★★★★★

[I tell you I am miserable,]
 Gongyla . . .
 in fact an omen . . .

[I dreamt that Hermes] appeared before me:
 'Lord,' I told him, 'I swear by the blessed goddess[†]
 that I can find no pleasure here on earth
 but I am possessed by a strange longing to die,
 to see the river at the gates of hell,
 whose banks are overgrown with lotus, wet with dew,
 the Acheron . . .'

★★★★★

[†]*the blessed goddess*: Aphrodite.

. . . already old age is wrinkling my
skin and my hair is turning from black
to grey; my knees begin to tremble
and my legs no longer carry me . . .
oh but once, once we were like young deer
. . . what can I do? . . .

                    . . . it is not possible
to return to my youth; for even
Eös, the dawn – whose arms are roses,
who brings light to the ends of the earth –
found that old age embraced Tithonus,
her immortal lover . . .

                    . . . I know I must die . . .
yet I love the tenderness of life
and this and desire keep me here in
the brightness and beauty of the sun
[and not with Hades . . .]

★★★★★

†The text of the peom is very fragmentary and much of this translation
is conjectural. *Eös, Tithonus*: Eös, the dawn goddess, fell in love with
Tithonus, a mortal. She asked Zues to give him immortality but forgot
to ask for eternal youth. Eventually he became old and shrivelled and
talked endlessly. Eös looked after him and finally turned him into the
cicada.

. . .frankly I wish that I were dead:
she was weeping as she took her leave from me

and many times she told me this:
'Oh what sadness we have suffered,
Sappho, for I'm leaving you against my will.'

So I gave this answer to her:
'Go, be happy but remember
me there, for you know how we have cherished you,

if not, then I would remind you
[of the joy we have known,] of all
the loveliness that we have shared together;

for many wreaths of violets,
of roses and of crocuses
. . . you wove around yourself by my side

. . . and many twisted garlands
which you had woven from the blooms
of flowers, you placed around your slender neck

. . . and you were annointed with
a perfume, scented with blossom,
. . .although it was fit for a queen

and on a bed, soft and tender
. . . you satisfied your desire . . .'

★★★★★

[. . . Atthis,]
although she is in Sardis,
her thoughts often stray here, to us . . .

[. . .for you know that she honoured] you
as if you were a goddess
and, most of all, delighted in your song.

But now she surpasses all the women
of Lydia, like the moon,
rose-fingered, after the sun has set,

shining brighter than all the stars; its light
stretches out over the salt–
filled sea and the fields brimming with flowers:

the beautiful dew falls and the roses
and the delicate chervil
and many-flowered honey-clover bloom.

But wandering here and there, she recalls
gentle Atthis with desire
and her tender heart is heavy with grief . . .

★★★★★

34

Atthis, you have come to hate the thought of me;
these days, you fly to Andromeda instead

★★★★★

35

Once upon a time, I loved you, Atthis,

yes, long ago . . .
even when I thought of you as a small

and graceless girl . . .

★★★★★

36

You have forgotten me;
oh, who in the world
          do you love better than me?

★★★★★

37

         How could
some yokel cast a spell on your heart –
doesn't she wear some yokel costume
and have no idea how to lift
her rags above her ankles?

★★★★★

38[†]

The moon has set
          and the stars have faded,
midnight has gone,
          long hours pass by, pass by;
I sleep alone

★★★★★

[†]One of Sappho's most famous fragments, although many scholars argue against her authorship.

I want to tell you something but shame prevents me . . .

if you truly desired something honest and good
and your tongue were not concocting something evil,
there would be no shame in your eyes
and you would plead your cause outright . . .

★★★★★

†Aristotle claimed that this fragment was a dialogue between Sappho
and her male contemporary, Alcaeus. The first line has been seen as part
of Alcaeus's speech and the rest as Sappho's reply. There is no other
evidence to support this claim and here, as in other translations, I have
concentrated on the actual evidence of the text rather than later
interpretations.

Mother dear, I simply cannot weave my cloth;
                              I'm overpowered
by desire for a slender young man – and it's
                              Aphrodite's fault

★★★★★

41

If you really love me,
choose a younger wife;

for I, being older,
could not bear to live
[with a younger man . . .]

★★★★★

42

Andromeda has been repaid

in full

★★★★★

43

Irana!
Never before have I found you so tiresome

★★★★★

44

I have had quite enough

of Gorgo

★★★★★

45

[Gorgo!]
Many greetings to the daughter

of so many kings[†]

★★★★★

46

Micca . . . I won't allow it . . .
you prefer the love of women

descended   from   Penthilus . . .[‡]

★★★★★

47

[I cannot bear it;]
. . . Archeanassa

is Gorgo's lover . . .

★★★★★

[†]*of so many kings*: the Greek is a pun on the family name, Polyanactidae, one of the rival aristocratic factions in Mytilene.

[‡]*Penthilus*: a mythical hero from whom the Penthilidae, another of the rival family factions at Mytilene, claimed descent.

48

I don't know what to do –

               I'm torn in two

★★★★★

49

I desire and yearn

           [for you]

★★★★★

50

Pain drips

       through me

★★★★★

51

You burn me

★★★★★

52

As long as you wish

★★★★★

53

. . . remember . . .
. . . we did the same
in our youth . . .

★★★★★

54

[When I was young and in love,]
I too wove garlands

★★★★★

– IV –
MARRIAGE

55

A honey-voiced woman
                    [sang at the wedding]

★★★★★

56

. . . take up your lyre;
                sing of the bride
                whose dress is violet . . .

★★★★★

57

[. . . sing of] the bride
                whose feet are graceful . . .

★★★★★

58

. . . we are going

to a wedding . . .

★★★★★

59

. . . all night long, [at your door,
bridegroom,] women sang of the love
between you and your bride whose dress
is the colour of violets;

but come now, wake up; go and fetch
the young men, your companions;
tonight we shall see no more sleep
than the clear-voiced nightingale

★★★★★

60

Beautiful woman
       graceful bride

★★★★★

61

'We give this woman away,'
              her father said

★★★★★

Lucky bridegroom,
the marriage you have prayed for has come to pass
and the bride you dreamed of is yours . . .

Beautiful bride,
to look at you gives joy; your eyes are like honey,
love flows over your gentle face . . .

Aphrodite
has honoured you above all others

★★★★★

Bridegroom,
          no woman was ever lovelier
                    [than your bride]

★★★★★

64

To what, my dear bridegroom, should I compare you best?
I should compare you best to a slender sapling

★★★★★

65†

Raise up the rooftop
(shout hymen!)
higher, carpenters,
(shout hymen!)
here comes the bridegroom, Ares' equal
and taller than the tallest giant

★★★★★

66

The door-keeper's feet are seven yards long
and his shoes were stitched from five ox-hides;
ten cobblers worked day and night to make them

★★★★★

†*65 and 66* have often been cited by scholars as evidence of Sappho's
heavy-handed sense of humour and lack of subtlety. Yet they are
important evidence of Sappho's celebration of women's experience.
The poems were probably sung as the bridal procession moved from
the bride's to the groom's house, at the climax of the ceremony. The
comparison of the groom in *65* to Ares, the god of war, and the ridicule
of his heroic stature satirizes male values. Again, in *66*, the door-keeper
was a friend of the groom who guarded the groom's house against the
ritual attempt of the bride's attendants to 'rescue' her.

Farewell, bride, farewell,
                    farewell, honoured bridegroom

★★★★★

68

　　　　　. . . like the sweet-apple
turning red at the top of the highest branch,
forgotten by the apple gatherers – no,
not quite forgotten, for they could not reach so far . .

★

　　　　　. . . like the hyacinth
on the mountains which shepherds tread under foot,
staining the earth with its purple flower . . .

★★★★★

69

[Why am I unhappy?]
Am I still longing
                    for my lost virginity?

★★★★★

70

[I assure you:]
I will remain a virgin
                    for ever

★★★★★

71

BRIDE: Virginity, virginity,
                    have you deserted me, where have you gone?

VIRGINITY: I will never return to you again,
                    never return to you again

★★★★★

The Marriage of Hector and Andromache

A herald came. . . . Idaeus . . . swift messenger . . .

'Hector and his companions are bringing a woman
with sparkling eyes, graceful Andromache, from sacred
Thebe,
from the ever-flowing streams of Placia, in their ships
across the salt-filled sea;
and with her they also carry
many golden bracelets, purple clothing, engraved trinkets,
ivory and silver goblets too numerous to count.'
This was Idaeus' speech.
And Hector's beloved father[†]
quickly leapt up and the story spread through the wide city
to those who held Hector dear.
At once the sons of Ilus[‡]
yoked mules to broad-wheeled carts and a crowd of women
and girls
whose ankles were slim, climbed on, while the daughters of
Priam . . .

. . . and the sweet music of the flute was mingled with the
clash
of castanets and the young women sang a sacred song
so clearly that their wondrous echo reached the sky . . .

. . . and in the streets, the mingled scents of myrrh and cassia
and frankincense;
with one voice the elder women shouted
for joy and with a clear cry all the men called on Paean,[§]
the noble archer, the skilled lyre player and they all sang
in praise of Hector and Andromache who were like gods

*****

[†]*beloved father*: Priam, king of Troy. [‡]*Ilus*: founder of Troy.
[§]*Paean*: the god, Apollo.

A bowl of ambrosia
was mixed with water.

Hermes took up the pitcher,
served wine to the gods.

Then they all raised their goblets
and poured libations

and they offered the bridegroom
all kind of blessings

★★★★★

– V –
MOTHER
AND
DAUGHTER

. . . my mother [used to say that]
in her youth it was thought to be
very fine to bind up your hair

with a dark purple [headband] – yes,
extremely fine indeed, although
for a girl whose hair is golden

like a torch flame [better] to wreathe
in it garlands of fresh flowers;
recently [I saw] a headband,

brightly coloured, from Sardis . . .

but for you, Cleis,[†] I do not have
a brightly coloured headband nor
do I know where I may find one . . .

★★★★★

[†]*Cleis*: according to one ancient biography, the name of both Sappho's
mother and her daughter.

75

I have a beautiful daughter, golden
like a flower, my beloved Cleis,
for her, in her place, I would not accept
the whole of Lydia, nor lovely . . .

★★★★★

76

There is no place for grief, [Cleis,]†
in a house which serves the Muse;
our own is no exception

★★★★★

77

[I once saw]
  a gentle little girl
                gathering flowers

★★★★★

†*Cleis*: Maximus of Tyre who quotes this fragment, records that it is
addressed to Sappho's daughter.

– VI –
THE
GODDESS
OF
LOVE

Immortal, Aphrodite, on your patterned throne,
daughter of Zeus, guile-weaver,
I beg you, goddess, don't subjugate my heart
with anguish, with grief

but come here to me now, if ever in the past
you have heard my distant pleas
and listened; leaving your father's golden house
you came to me then

with your chariot yoked; beautiful swift sparrows
brought you around the dark earth
with a whirl of wings, beating fast, from heaven
down through the mid-air

to reach me quickly; then you, my sacred goddess,
your immortal face smiling,
asked me what had gone wrong this time and this time
why was I begging

and what in my demented heart, I wanted most:
'Who shall I persuade this time
to take you back, yet once again, to her love;
who wrongs you, Sappho?

For if she runs away, soon she shall run after,
if she shuns gifts, she shall give,
if she does not love you, soon she shall even
against her own will.'

So come to me now, free me from this aching pain,
fulfil everything that
my heart desires to be fulfilled: you, yes you,
will be my ally.

★★★★★

Leave Crete and come to me here, to this holy temple,
where the loveliness of your apple grove
waits for you and your altars smoulder
with burning frankincense;

there, far away beyond the apple branches, cold streams
murmur, roses shade every corner
and, when the leaves rustle, you are seized
by a strange drowsiness;

there, a meadow, a pasture for horses, blooms with all
the flowers of Spring, while the breezes blow
so gently . . .

there . . . Cyprian goddess, take and pour
gracefully like wine into golden cups,
a nectar mingled with all the joy
of our celebrations

★★★★★

[Cypris and] Nereids,† grant that my brother ‡
will return here to me without harm and that
everything which he wishes for in his heart
will come to pass;

grant that he atone for all his former crimes
and become a joy to his friends, a torment
to his enemies and let no one ever cause
us grief again;

grant too that he may wish his sister to have
her share of honour, and wretched sorrow . . .

★★★★★

†*Cypris and Nereids*: Cypris: Aphrodite, invoked as goddess of the sea.
Nereids: sea-nymphs.

‡*brother*: some ancient sources name Sappho's brother as Charaxus, a
wine-merchant. This fragment might well refer to the political troubles
in Mytilene during Sappho's lifetime and to her family's involvement in
them.

. . . may she find even you, Cypris, too severe
and, as for Doricha,† may she never boast
that she returned for a second time
to the love she had longed for

★★★★★

†*Doricha*: according to the historian, Herodotus, Charaxus, Sappho's
brother, fell in love with and freed a courtesan of Naucratis, called
Rhodopis. When he returned to Mytilene, Herodotus continued, his
sister ridiculed him in verse. Several centuries later, another ancient
writer, Strabo, wrote that Sappho called Rhodopis, Doricha, although
yet another, Athenaeus, rejected this. Modern scholars usually accept
Strabo's comment and identify this fragment as Sappho's poem against
her brother. The evidence of the sources is slight and that of the tiny
fragment even slighter; the gender of the subject of the verbs is not even
clear in the Greek. It seems as likely that this is part of a prayer to
Aphrodite, similar to 78, in which Sappho begs for help in a love affair.

82

[Aphrodite, come to me]
  whether you are at Cyprus

                    or Paphos

                              or Panormus

★★★★★

83

  Aphrodite,
  your garlands are made of golden leaves;

  if only I
  could have a share in such good fortune

★★★★★

84

  [Goddess of love,]
    to you I will sacrifice

                    a white goat

★★★★★

85

Sappho,
why spurn Aphrodite

              whose blessings are many?

★★★★★

86

In a dream
I spoke with Aphrodite

                    the Cyprian goddess
                    ★★★★★

87

[She said to me:]
'Sappho, you and my servant, Eros . . .'
                    ★★★★★

88†

          [Eros came down from heaven,]
his dark purple cloak
wrapped around him . . .
                    ★★★★★

89†

          [Eros, the god of desire,]
          brings pain

                    weaves tales
[for mortals . . .]
                    ★★★★★

90

Persuasion is

                    Aphrodite's daughter;

it is she who beguiles
                    our mortal hearts
                    ★★★★★

†88 and 89: the ancient sources which quote these fragments, Pollux and Maximus of Tyre, comment that they are descriptions of Eros.

– VII –
RELIGION

Appear to me, lady Hera,[†] I beg you,
reveal your graceful form; for it was you who
once answered the prayers of the Atridae,[‡]
illustrious kings;

after many adventures, near Troy, at sea,
they came here, to Lesbos, but they could not leave,
could not complete their journey home until
they had summoned you

and Zeus, suppliants' god and Dionysus,
Thyone's lovely son; so be gracious now,
send your help to me now as you have helped
others in the past . . .

★★★★★

[†]*Hera*: goddess who represents women, worshipped on Lesbos where, at her annual festival, female beauty was celebrated.

[‡]*Atridae*: a reference to an incident in the *Odyssey* (3.130ff). The Atridae are the sons of Atreus, king of Mycenae – Menelaus, king of Sparta, husband of Helen; and Agamemnon, the commander-in-chief of the Greek forces at Troy. On their way home to Greece after the Trojan War, the brothers quarrelled; Menelaus thought it best to sail home immediately while Agamemnon stayed in Troy. Menelaus came to Lesbos where he prayed to Zeus for guidance. In Sappho's poem, Agamemnon does not argue with Menelaus but is present on Lesbos. The brothers do not pray only to Zeus but also to Hera and Dionysus, the other deities particularly worshipped on Lesbos.

92

When the full moon rose
women took their place
around the altar . . .

★★★★★

93

[. . . they were dancing]
as Cretan women once danced
beside a lovely altar,
their graceful feet treading down
the smooth soft bloom of the grass

★★★★★

94

Alas for Adonis

★★★★★

95

Gentle Adonis is dying, Cytherea,[†]
what should we do?

Beat your breasts, young women, tear your tunics
[and mourn for him]

★★★★★

[†]*Cytherea*: Aphrodite, so called because the island of Cythera
in the Aegean was said to have been her birthplace.

96

They say that long ago
Leda† once found an egg;

it was the colour of
a hyacinth . . .

★★★★★

97

Leto and Niobe‡ were
the very best of friends

★★★★★

†*Leda*: in Greek mythology, wife of Tyndareus, king of Sparta and raped by Zeus in the form of a swan. She laid two eggs; from one was hatched the twins, Castor and Pollux, from the other, Helen of Troy.

‡*Leto and Niobe*: Leto: mother of the gods, Apollo and Artemis. Niobe: mother of seven daughters and seven sons, she boasted that she was therefore superior to Leto, although Leto's two children were divine. Apollo and Artemis then killed Niobe's children in revenge. Niobe wept for them continuously and became a column of stone from which her tears continued to flow

– VIII –
POETRY
AND THE
MUSES

98

My dearest friends
today I will sing with a clear voice
            to enchant you all

★★★★★

99

Come, my lovely tortoise-shell lyre;
my music will give you speech

★★★★★

100[†]

My words may only be of air
            but they will always give pleasure

★★★★★

101

The singer from Lesbos
surpasses all of those
                  from other lands

★★★★★

[†]This fragment is quoted by Edmonds and comes from a painting of
Sappho on an Attic vase c.430B.C.

Come here, to me, rose-like Graces;
                         Muses, [bind up] your lovely hair

★★★★★

   Arms like roses,
                         daughters of Zeus,
   sacred Graces,
                         come to me here

★★★★★

Come here to me, to me, Muses;
                         leave your golden house

★★★★★

[It is the Muses]
> who have brought me honour
> through the gift of their art

★★★★★

106

[Sappho said:]

The Muses have made me happy
in my lifetime

and when I die
I shall never be forgotten[†]

★★★★★

[†]According to ancient commentators, Sappho was the first to say that
poetry brings the poet immortality.

When you die, you will lie unremembered for ever more;
for you there will be no regret, no share in the roses
of Pieria; invisible in Hades, as on earth,
you will wander aimlessly among the unknown dead . . .

★★★★★

†Stobaeus quoted this fragment and claimed that it was addressed to a
woman of no education. Plutarch also wrote that it was to a rich
woman or an ignorant woman, without culture. Modern commenta-
tors cite it as an example of Sappho's bitchiness. However, as the
fragment stands, its tone is as much elegiac as satirical.

. . . but now my dear friends

[let us end our song;]
it is almost day . . .

★★★★★

– IX –
NATURE

109

[The evening star –]
the most beautiful
of all the stars

★★★★★

110

Hesperus, you bring everything that
the light-tinged dawn has scattered;

you bring the sheep, you bring the goat, you bring
the child back to its mother

★★★★★

111

The stars around the lovely moon
hide their brightness when it is full
and shines the clearest over all
the earth

★★★★★

112†

[The moon is]
                    like silver

★★★★★

†This fragment may well be part of a simile, like that in *33*, which compares the beauty of a woman who surpasses her companions to the moon outshining the stars.

113

Golden broom grew
                          along the shore

★★★★★

114

The nightingale is
                          the harbinger of Spring
                          and her voice is desire

★★★★★

115†

[. . . like frightened doves]
    whose hearts turn to ice
                          whose wings falter . . .

★★★★★

†This fragment is quoted in a commentary on Pindar which says that it comes from a description of doves.

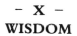

– X –
WISDOM

116

Death must be an evil – and the gods agree;
for why else would they live for ever?

★★★★★

117

Gold is the child of the gods;
it will never decay
and cannot be corrupted

★★★★★

118

[Sappho's advice was:]
  when someone sows anger in your heart,
keep quiet;
        curb your thoughtless, barking tongue

★★★★★

119

Beauty endures only for as long as it can be seen;
goodness, beautiful today, will remain so tomorrow

★★★★★

120

  Wealth without virtue is
                a harmful companion;
    but a mixture of both,
              the happiest friendship

★★★★★

GLOSSARY

Acheron, one of the rivers of the lower world of the dead.

Achilles, son of Peleus and Thetis, one of the commanders of the Greek forces at Troy and the hero of the *Iliad*.

Actaeon, a keen huntsman, he spied on the goddess Artemis while she was bathing naked in a pool and was turned by her into a stag and torn to pieces by his own hounds.

Adonis, a beautiful youth loved by Aphrodite. He was killed, while hunting, by a boar. Aphrodite persuaded Zeus, the king of the gods, to restore him to life but Persephone, the queen of the lower world, who was also in love with him, refused to let him go. Zeus decreed that he should spend half the year in the lower world and the other half on earth. A fertility cult, popular with women, was associated with his death and rebirth, first in the East and then in Greece.

Aegean sea, between Greece and Asia Minor.

Alyattes, king of Lydia c.610–560B.C., founder of the Lydian Empire.

Amorgos, small island in the Aegean, home of the poet Semonides.

Andromache, daughter of Eëtion, king of Thebe and wife of Hector, prince of Troy.

Aphrodite, goddess of love and beauty, she sprang from the foam of the sea near Paphos in Cyprus or on the shore of Cythera, an Aegean island, hence her names, Cypris, Cytherea and Cyprogeneia (Cyprus-born).

Apollo, son of Leto and Zeus, sister of Artemis, god of music, archery, prophecy, medicine and youth. He was also associated with the sun

105

and in Greek art was portrayed as the epitome of youthful male beauty. See note on No. 97.

Ares, god of war.

Artemis, daughter of Leto and Zeus, sister of Apollo, a virgin moon goddess who had many aspects but was particularly associated with animals and wild places. See note on No. 97.

Asia Minor, modern Turkey.

Atridae, the brothers, Menelaus and Agamemnon, sons of Atreus, king of Mycenae. Menelaus married Helen and became king of Sparta, while Agamemnon married her sister, Clytemnestra. When Helen was abducted by Paris, Prince of Troy, they raised a Greek army to besiege the city with Agamemnon as its commander-in-chief. See note on No. 91.

Charaxus, according to some ancient biographers, Sappho's brother and a wine-merchant. See note on No. 80.

Chiron, a centaur (half-man, half-horse), tutor to Achilles.

Cleanactidae, aristocratic family faction in Mytilene during Sappho's lifetime, of which the tyrant Myrsilus was a member.

Cleis, Sappho's daughter and, according to some sources, also the name of her mother.

Crete, island in the south Aegean, associated with the worship of Aphrodite.

Cypris, see *Aphrodite*.

Cyprus, island in the eastern Mediterranean, the birthplace and haunt of Aphrodite.

Cytherea, see *Aphrodite*.

Dionysus, son of Thyone and Zeus and the god of the vine, fertility and poetry.

Eös, the dawn, lover of Tithonus. See note on No. 31.

Eros, god of sexual desire, the attendant of Aphrodite.

Graces, companions of Aphrodite, three goddesses of beauty and charm.

Hades, god of death, king of the lower world.

Hector, prince of Troy, son of Priam and husband of Andromache.

Helen of Troy, queen of Sparta, wife of Menelaus and famous for her great beauty. In the *Iliad*, her abduction by Paris, prince of Troy, starts the war between Greece and Troy. After a ten-year siege of the city, she is recaptured by the victorious Greeks and returns to Sparta.

Hera, queen of the gods and Zeus' consort, she represents women, their lives, sexuality and occupations and was particularly worshipped on Lesbos. See note on No. 91.

Hermes, messenger of the gods who conducts the souls of the dead to the lower world.

Hermione, daughter of Menelaus and Helen.

Hesperus, the evening star, depicted in Greek art as a young boy carrying a torch.

Idaeus, a stock name for Trojans in classical literature. In No. 72, Idaeus is the name of the messenger who announces the arrival of Hector and Andromache at Troy.

Iliad, epic poem, attributed to Homer and probably composed in the eighth century B.C., which relates incidents of the Trojan War.

Ilus, the founder of Troy or Ilium. Trojans are sometimes referred to in literature as the sons or daughters of Ilus. See note on No. 72.

Leda, mother of Helen. See note on No. 96.

Lesbos, island in the western Aegean, off the coast of Asia Minor, home of Sappho.

Leto, mother of Apollo and Artemis. See note on No. 97.

Lydia, a rich and powerful kingdom of Asia Minor.

Menelaus, king of Sparta and husband of Helen. See note on No. 91.

Muses, nine goddesses of literature, music and dance, connected with poetic inspiration.

Myrsilus, member of the Cleanactidae, one of the feuding aristocratic factions in Mytilene during Sappho's lifetime. He became tyrant of Mytilene in the early sixth century B.C.

Naucratis, port of the Nile delta, centre of contact between Greece and Egypt. See note on No 81.

Nereids, sea-nymphs, daughters of Nereus, the sea-god.

Niobe, turned to stone after her children were killed by Apollo and Artemis. See note on No. 97.

Odysseus, king of Ithaca, a small island off the west coast of Greece and one of the Greek leaders of Troy, famous for his cunning.

Odyssey, epic poem attributed to Homer, probably composed in the eighth century B.C. It relates the ten-year adventures of Odysseus as he journeys home from Troy to Ithaca.

Paean, a hymn addressed to Apollo. In No. 72 Sappho refers to Apollo himself as Paean.

Pandora, in Hesiod's poetry, the first woman on earth, created by Zeus as a punishment for the theft of fire by the demi-god, Prometheus. Pandora brought with her a box which she was forbidden to open but, overcome by curiosity, she did so and released all the evils of the world, trapping Hope inside when she quickly replaced the lid. According to Hesiod, Pandora and all other members of her sex are responsible for man's sufferings.

Panormus, a city mentioned in No. 82 as a haunt of Aphrodite; its location is unknown.

Paphos, a town near the coast of southern Cyprus, reputed to be the place where Aphrodite emerged from the foam of the sea and famous as a centre for her worship.

Paris, prince of Troy, brother of Hector, son of Priam. In the *Iliad*, his abduction of Helen from Sparta to Troy causes the war between Greece and Troy.

Peleus, husband of the sea-nymph, Thetis, and father of the Greek hero, Achilles.

Penelope, queen of Ithaca and wife of Odysseus. In the *Odyssey*, she rules Ithaca in his absence at Troy and is wooed by several suitors but remains faithfull to Odysseus and waits patiently for his return.

Penthilidae, one of the rival families in Mytilene during Sappho's time, who claimed that they were the descendants of the mythical hero, Penthilus. In No. 46, Sappho mentions them with disapproval.

Phaon, a legendary boatman of Lesbos, said by some ancient sources to be the subject of Sappho's unrequited love.

Pieria, a district of northern Greece, birthplace of the Muses.

Pittacus, of Mytilene c.650–570B.C. He commanded the army in the war against Athenian colonists at Sigeum and killed the enemy leader in mortal combat. With Alcaeus, he was involved in a plot to overthrow the tyrant, Myrsilus, but changed sides, betrayed his companions and later became tyrant himself.

Placia, river near Thebe in Cilicia, a district of southern Asia Minor.

Polyanactidae, aristocratic faction in Mytilene. See note on No. 45.

Priam, father of Hector and king of Troy during the Trojan War. See note on No. 72.

Rhodopis, courtesan of Naucratis, loved by Sappho's brother, Charaxus, and associated by Strabo with Doricha. See note on No. 81.

Sardis, chief city of Lydia.

Sicyon, Greek city in the Peloponnese, home of the woman poet Praxilla.

Sigeum, promontory near Troy, colonized by Athenians c.600B.C. and the subject of a war between Athens and Lesbos who both claimed territorial rights.

Socrates, Greek philosopher who lived in Athens 469–399B.C. He taught philosophy to a group of young men, including Plato whose dialogues feature Socrates and his teachings. He was executed in 399B.C. for corrupting the youth of the city.

Sparta, Greek city in the Peloponnese, in mythology ruled by Menelaus and Helen.

Thebe, city in Cilicia, a district of southern Asia Minor.

Thera, Greek island in the southern Aegean.

Thetis, sea-nymph, daughter of Nereus the god of the sea. She was married to Peleus and had a son, Achilles, the Greek hero of the Trojan War.

Thyone, or Semele, mother of the god Dionysus.

Tithonus, the mortal lover of Eös, the dawn. See note on No. 31.

Troy, city in northern Asia Minor. In the *Iliad*, it is besieged by a Greek army for ten years and then destroyed by them in revenge for the abduction of Helen from Sparta by Paris.

Zeus, king of the gods.

Sappho's Companions

Anactoria:	No. 21
Andromeda:	34, 42
Archeanassa:	47, 35
Atthis:	18, 33, 34
Dicca:	16
Doricha:	81
Gongyla:	22, 30
Gorgo:	44, 45, 47
Gyrinno:	17
Irana:	43
Micca:	46
Mnasidica:	17

Ancient Writers and Sources Mentioned in the Text

Aelian, rhetorician and writer. c.A.D.170–235.
Alcaeus, lyric poet of Mytilene, contemporary of Sappho, c.620–580B.C.
Anacreon, lyric poet, c.575–490B.C.
Aristophanes, comic playwright, c.450–385B.C.
Aristotle, philosopher, 384–322B.C.
Athenaeus, writer, *fl*.c.A.D.200.

Corinna, lyric woman poet, possibly fifth century B.C.

Dioscorides, epigrammatist, late third century B.C.

Eusebius, Christian historian, c.A.D.260–340.

Herodotus, historian, fifth century B.C.
Hesiod, epic poet, c.700B.C.
Homer, name given by the Greeks to the author of the epic poems, the *Iliad* and the *Odyssey*, although it is not even known whether they have a joint authorship. They were probably composed in the eighth century B.C and reached their final form c.700B.C.
Horace, Latin poet, 65–08B.C.

Maximus of Tyre, philosopher and rhetorician, c.A.D.125–185.
Myrtis, lyric woman poet, fifth century B.C.

Ovid, Latin poet, 43B.C.–A.D.17.

Palatine Anthology, compiled c.A.D.980 of ealier Greek epigrams.
Parian Marble, a stone slab inscribed with a summary of Greek history up to 264/3B.C.
Pausanias, traveller and geographer, *fl.* c.A.D.150.
Philostratus, philosopher and writer, c.A.D.170–247.
Pindar, choral lyric poet, 518–438B.C.
Plato, philosopher, c.429–347B.C.
Plutarch, biographer, moralist and essayist, first century A.D.
Pollux, lexicographer and rhetorician, second century A.D.
Porphyrion, commentator on Horace, third century A.D.
Praxilla, lyric woman poet, *fl.* 451B.C.

Semonides, iambic and elegaic poet, mid-seventh century B.C.
Solon, Athenian poet and statesman, c.600B.C.
Stobaeus, anthologist, carly fifth century A.D.
Suda, an encyclopaedia, compiled in the tenth century A.D.

Zenobius, rhetorician, second century A.D.

CHRONOLOGICAL TABLE

Date	Event	Literature
776B.C.	First Olympic Games	
750		Homer
		Semonides
700		Hesiod
687	Kingdom of Lydia founded by Gyges	
655–585	Tyranny at Corinth	
620–570	War between Lesbos and Athenian colonists at Sigeum	Sappho and Alcaeus
	Tyranny at Mytilene: Pittacus, Alcaeus, Myrsilus	
610–560	Alyattes king of Lydia	
595	Earliest Greek coins minted	
594/3	Solon codifies Athenian law and makes constitutional reforms which lay down the foundation of the democratic state	Solon
582–573	Pythian, Isthmian and Nemean Games	
572	established	
	Marriage contest for Agariste, daughter of Cleisthenes, tyrant of Sicyon	
561–514	Tyranny at Athens	
		Anacreon

508/7	Cleisthenes makes further democratic reforms at Athens	
		Myrtis
		Corinna
		Pindar
490	First Persian expedition against Greece defeated at the battle of Marathon	
480	Second Persian invasion, again defeated	Herodotus
461	Ephialtes makes radical democratic reforms at Athens	Tragedy at Athens:
459–454	First Peloponnesian War between Athens and Sparta	Aeschylus Sophocles Euripides
451	Pericles' law at Athens restricting citizenship to men whose parents are both Athenian	Praxilla
431–404	Second Peloponnesian War between Athens and Sparta	Aristophanes
411–410 and 404	Right-wing revolutions at Athens overthrow the democracy and establish an oligarchy	Plato
399	Socrates executed at Athens by the restored democracy	
343	Aristotle at Macedon as tutor to Alexander	Aristotle
338	Athens defeated by Philip of Macedon	
336	Alexander becomes king of Macedon	

SELECT BIBLIOGRAPHY

Arthur, Marilyn, 'Liberated Women: The Classical Era', in Bridenthal, R., and Koonz, C. (eds), *Becoming Visible: Women in European History*, Houghton Mifflin Company (Boston 1977), 60–89

Boardman, John and La Rocca, E., *Eros in Greece*, Phaidon (London 1978)

Bowra, C.M., *Greek Lyric Poetry*, 2nd ed., Oxford University Press (Oxford 1961)

*Burn, A.R., *The Lyric Age of Greece*, Edward Arnold (London 1978)

Campbell, David A. (ed.) (1), *Greek Lyric Poetry*, Macmillan (London 1967 repr. 1976)

*(2) (ed.), *Greek Lyric I*, Loeb Classical Library (London 1982)

(3), *The Golden Lyre: The Themes of the Greek Lyric Poets*, Duckworth (London 1983)

Davison, J.A., *From Archilochus to Pindar*, Macmillan (London 1968)

Devereux, George, 'The Nature of Sappho's Seizure in fr. 31LP as Evidence of her Inversion', *Classical Quarterly* n.s. 20 (1970), 17–31

*Dover, K.J., *Greek Homosexuality*, Duckworth (London 1978)

duBois, Page, 'Sappho and Helen', *Arethusa* 11 (1978), 89–99

Fränkel, H., *Early Greek Poetry and Philosophy*, trans. M. Hadas and J. Willis, Blackwell (Oxford 1975)

Hallett, Judith, 'Sappho and her Social Context: Sense and Sensuality', *Signs* 4 (1979), 447–64

Jenkyns, Richard, *Three Classical Poets: Sappho, Catullus and Juvenal*,

Duckworth (London 1982)

*Lefkowitz, Mary R., *Heroines and Hysterics*, Duckworth (London 1981)
 *and Fant, Maureen B. (eds), *Women's Life in Greece and Rome: A Source Book in Translation*, Duckworth (London 1982)

Lesky, Albin, *A History of Greek Literature*, trans. J.Willis and C.de Heer, Methuen (London 1966)

McEvilley, Thomas, 'Sappho, fragment ninety-four', *Phoenix* 25 (1971), 1–11

Marcovich, M., 'Sappho fr.31: anxiety attack or love declaration?' *Classical Quarterly* n.s. 22 (1972), 19–32

Marry, John D., 'Sappho and the heroic ideal: *erotos arete*', *Arethusa* 12 (1979), 71–92

*Murray, Oswyn, *Early Greece*, Fontana (London 1980)

*Page, Denys, *Sappho and Alcaeus*, Oxford University Press (Oxford 1955, repr. 1979)

*Pomeroy, Sarah, *Goddesses, Whores, Wives and Slaves: Women in Classical Antiquity*, Schocken Books (New York 1975)

Robinson, David M., *Sappho and her Influence*, Harrap (London 1925)

Tsagarakis, Odysseus, *Self-expression in Early Greek Lyric, Elegiac and Iambic Poetry*, Steiner (Wiesbaden 1977)

Wilamowitz-Moellendorff, Ulrich von, *Sappho und Simonides* (Berlin 1913)

Wright, F.A., 'The Women Poets of Greece', *Fortnightly Review* 113 (February 1923), 323–33

*Recommended further reading (paperback and/or widely available)

KEY TO THE FRAGMENTS (1)

Translations	Lobel and Page	Translations	Lobel and Page	Translations	Lobel and Page	Translations	Lobel and Page
1	47	31	58	61	109	91	17
2	130	32	94	62	112	92	154
3	138	33	96	63	113	93	i.a. 16
4	46	34	131	64	115	94	168
5	i.a. 25	35	49	65	111	95	140a
6	147	36	129	66	110a	96	166
7	146	37	57	67	116 and 117	97	142
8	52	38	976PMG	68	105a and c	98	160
9	145	39	137	69	107	99	118
10	120	40	102	70	152E	100	1aE
11	41	41	121	71	114	101	106
12	126	42	133	72	44	102	128
13	149 and 151	43	91	73	141	103	53
14	23	44	144	74	98a and b	104	127
15	56	45	155	75	132	105	32
16	81b	46	71 ll.1–3	76	150	106	193
17	82a	47	213 ll.1–2	77	122	107	55
18	8	48	51	78	1	108	43 ll.8–9
19	i.a. 13	49	36	79	2	109	104b
20	31	50	37	80	5	110	104a
21	16	51	38	81	15b	111	34
22	22	52	45	82	35	112	34
23	156 and 167	53	24a ll.2–4	83	33	113	143
24	100	54	125	84	40	114	136
25	39	55	185 and 153	85	133	115	42
26	48	56	21 ll.11–13	86	134	116	201
27	197	57	i.a. 26	87	159	117	204
28	123	58	27 l.8	88	54	118	158
29	26 ll.2–4	59	30	89	172 and 188	119	50
30	95	60	108	90	200; 90; 33E	120	148

KEY TO THE FRAGMENTS (2)

Lobel and Page	Translations	Lobel and Page	Translations	Lobel and Page	Translations	Lobel and Page	Translations
1	78	49	35	114	71	148	120
2	79	50	119	115	64	149	13
5	80	51	48	116	67	150	76
8	18	52	8	117	67	151	13
15b	81	53	103	118	99	153	55
16	21	54	88	120	10	154	92
17	91	55	107	121	41	155	45
21 ll.11–13	56	56	15	122	77	156	23
22	22	57	37	123	28	158	118
23	14	58	31	125	54	159	87
24a ll.2–4	53	71 ll.1–3	46	126	12	160	98
26 ll.2–4	29	81b	16	127	104	166	96
27 l.8	58	82a	17	128	102	167	23
30	59	90	90	129	36	168	94
31	20	91	43	130	2	172	89
32	105	94	32	131	34	185	55
33	83	95	30	132	75	188	89
34	111 and 112	96	33	133	42 and 85	193	106
35	82	98a and b	74	134	86	197	27
36	49	100	24	136	114	200	90
37	50	102	40	137	39	201	116
38	51	104a	110	138	3	204	117
39	25	104c	109	140a	95	213 lll–2	47
40	84	105a and c	68	141	73	i.a. 13	19
41	11	106	101	142	97	i.a. 16	93
42	115	107	69	143	113	i.a. 25	5
43 ll.8–9	108	108	60	144	44	i.a. 26	57
44	72	109	61	145	9	1aE	100
45	52	110a	66	146	7	33E	90
46	4	111	65	147	6	152E	70
47	1	112	62			976PMG	38
48	26	113	63				